FACE TO FACE WITH
BUTTERFLIES

by Darlyne A. Murawski

NATIONAL
GEOGRAPHIC
WASHINGTON D.C.

FACE TO FACE

You've probably read the story of the very hungry caterpillar. But what do adult butterflies do when *they* get really hungry? These delicate-looking creatures can turn into big bullies. Believe it or not, they sometimes have food fights! I got to see this for myself back when I was working on my graduate research in a Costa Rican rain forest.

It was the dry season, and many of the plants had stopped flowering. The butterflies needed the sweet nectar from the flowers to survive. So they started

➡️ *Two* Heliconius *butterflies with numbers on their wings visit flowers in Costa Rica.*

⬇️ *This cut-away view of a tubular flower reveals a butterfly reaching the tip of its proboscis* (pro-BAH-sis) *to the base, where the nectar is.*

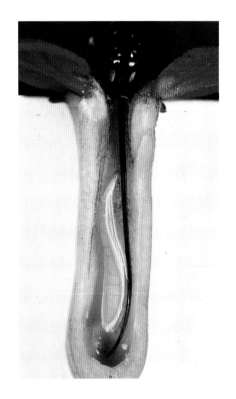

fighting over the few flowers left. Sometimes one butterfly would hold tight to a single flower—it could stay there all morning, sucking every last drop of nectar. Another butterfly would approach and pounce on the first butterfly's open wings, trying to knock it off. It kicked, shoved, and even head-butted the other butterfly, trying to claim the flower all to itself.

I was part of a group studying passion vine butterflies. I studied their role in pollinating certain plants. Each of us researched a different part of the butterflies' lives. With a net, we'd catch a butterfly and then use a permanent marker to write an identification number on its wing. We'd jot down information about it, then release it. That way we could keep track of it.

↑ *My colleague, Mauricio Linares, catches passion vine butterflies with a long-handled net in the Cauca Valley of Colombia (South America).*

By patrolling areas where the butterflies lived, then catching them, taking notes about them, and releasing them, we could learn many things. We could see how long they lived, what plants they had collected pollen from, where they slept at night, and how the population changed over time.

Some butterflies had their own way of doing things and their own daily routines. They learned the locations of their favorite flowers, host plants, and places to sleep at night. They would return to those places day after day. But they had to be flexible too, because their environment was always changing.

I was happy to see certain butterflies over and over again when I made my rounds. It was like running in to old friends.

MEET

A red lacewing butterfly (Cethosia biblis) *spreads its two pairs of colorful wings as it drinks nectar from a flower.*

THE BUTTERFLY

A close-up of a butterfly's *wing shows thousands of colorful, overlapping scales attached to the surface. The raised diagonal lines are the tube-like veins of the wing.*

Have you ever caught a butterfly and got powdery stuff on your fingers? This is actually many tiny scales, and a butterfly's wing is covered with thousands of them. The scales help to water-proof the insect's wings. They also give the butterfly its unique color pattern. Butterflies are part of a larger group (called an "order") of flying insects, the Lepidoptera (pronounced lep-i-DOP-ter-a). This term comes from the Greek words for "scaly wings."

The Lepidoptera consists of butterflies, skippers,

➡ *Tropical rain forest butterflies shown feeding:* **1** *A* Taygetis *butterfly drinks the juice of a rotting fruit. (Panama)* **2** *A male* Marpesia iole *butterfly sips water from the side of a stream. (Panama)*

HOW TO HANDLE A BUTTERFLY

DON'T
— Hold them by their wings.

— Handle them immediately after they emerge as adults.

DO
— Go underneath a resting butterfly and slowly and carefully tease it onto your hand or finger.

— Catch a butterfly in a net and observe it, or transfer it to a screened enclosure, then let it go.

3 *A male* Hamadryas feronia *butterfly laps up sweat on a person's arm. (Costa Rica)* 4 *A delicate* Pteronymia donella *butterfly sips juice from an insect carcass. (Colombia)*

and moths. Skippers are often grouped with butterflies. These groups share many traits in common, but the easiest way to tell them apart is by the shape of their antennae. In butterflies, the antennae are clubbed, or thickened on the ends. In skippers, the tip of each antenna looks like a hook. In most moths, antennae are feathery or straight, with no thickening on the tip.

Butterflies go through four very different stages during their lives: egg, larva, pupa (or chrysalis), and adult. The life cycle starts with an adult butterfly laying her eggs one at a time or in batches. She lays them on a leaf or stem of a plant called a host plant. For example, the host plant of a monarch butterfly is milkweed. Females can be very picky in choosing the right plant. They taste it first with their feet to make sure they select plants their offspring can eat.

The caterpillar (or larva) develops inside the egg.

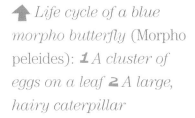
Life cycle of a blue morpho butterfly (Morpho peleides): **1** *A cluster of eggs on a leaf* **2** *A large, hairy caterpillar*

When it hatches, it's hungry! It can't drink, but it gobbles up solid foods like leaves, flowers, or stems—some species even eat other insects. As a caterpillar feeds and grows, it sheds, or molts, its outer skin about five times.

Next it becomes a pupa. The caterpillar's body turns to liquid inside. It undergoes a big change, or metamorphosis, and is transformed into the body of an adult butterfly (also called an imago). The pupa changes color as the adult develops inside.

When a new adult emerges from the chrysalis, it pumps body fluids through the soft veins of its crumpled wings until they fully expand. After a few hours, the wings are stiff enough to fly.

As adults, butterflies spend their time eating,

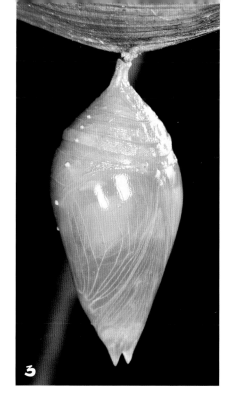

3 A newly formed green pupa 4 An adult blue morpho resting on a leaf

courting, mating, searching for host plants, laying eggs, and resting. They are cold-blooded. This means that their temperature changes to match the outside temperature. If they need to warm up, they bask in the sun or shiver, which generates heat. Most sleep upside down with their wings held together.

While caterpillars can only chew their food, adults can only sip liquids. They have a hollow proboscis that unrolls like a party favor for drinking, then curls up at rest. They use it like a straw to draw up liquids. Meals include nectar, rotting fruit, sap, bird droppings and fresh dung, urine, sweat, mud, tree sap, or insect carcasses. The salts deposited alongside streams can also attract lots of butterflies.

Butterfly eyes are made up of many smaller eyes. These compound eyes help butterflies sense movement in all directions and spot predators, potential mates, and sources of food.

Most adults have no sense of hearing, but they can sense sound vibrations through their wings. Some moths have ears. They can hear if a predator, such as a bat, is coming—giving them time to escape.

Butterflies smell odors with their antennae. Antennae are also used for balance and orientation in flight.

Courtship involves sending chemical messages. Butterflies, like most animals, can emit chemical signals called pheromones to attract a mate. The butterflies detect the pheromone scent with their antennae. If they can't see the other butterfly, they fly upwind, following the scent to its source. The adult female can choose to accept or reject the male. If she accepts him, the butterflies mate by joining their abdomens end to end. Once her eggs are fertilized,

1 Courtship: A male flutters above a female.
2 Mating: A male and female butterfly are attached by their abdomens while he fertilizes her eggs.
3 Egg laying: A female lays eggs on a host plant.

A collection of butterflies in a museum drawer. The specimens include information about species, location, date, and collector. Scientists learn a lot from collections like this.

the female looks for host plants on which to lay them.

Butterflies are a valuable part of the food web. As adults, they become food for other insects, birds, lizards, spiders, mammals, and fungi. Butterflies also carry pollen from one plant to another. Pollination enables the plant to develop fruit and seeds.

15

MIGRATION

What makes a butterfly fly thousands of miles, to a place it's never been before? How does it find its way? These are just a couple of the mysteries scientists are trying to unravel.

Many butterflies migrate because they have to. Sometimes there's no food when summer ends. Or it's too hot or crowded. They can fly a little ways or very far to reach their goal. Some even cross the ocean.

The most famous migrants are the monarchs. Each fall they travel up to 3,000 miles (4,828 km) from their

Monarchs (Danaus plexippus) *blanket a tree trunk in Mexico at the end of their long southward migration. They wait until spring to fly north to breed.*

In the fall, monarchs in the western part of North America fly to an area along the California coast. The largest migration, however, occurs in the eastern and midsection of the U.S. and Canada, where monarchs fly thousands of miles to spend the winter in certain mountaintops in Mexico. These migrating butterflies won't breed until spring.

1

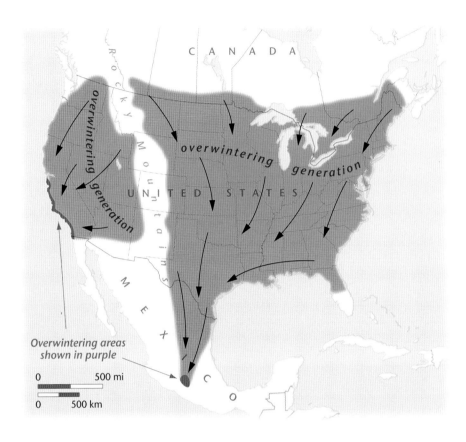

Overwintering areas
shown in purple

0   500 mi

0   500 km

A sample of other butterflies that migrate:
1 the yellow brimstone,
2 the white peacock,
3 the question mark,
and 4 the statira sulphur.

2

homes in Canada and the U.S. to Mexico and California. They use the fat in their bodies to give them energy to make the long trip and stop along the way to drink nectar. They spend the winter down south. In spring, they begin the journey back north. Along the way, they reproduce. Their offspring fly a bit farther. But the last generation of monarchs that emerge in late summer and early fall are different. They are the ones that head south to the winter roosts.

3

18

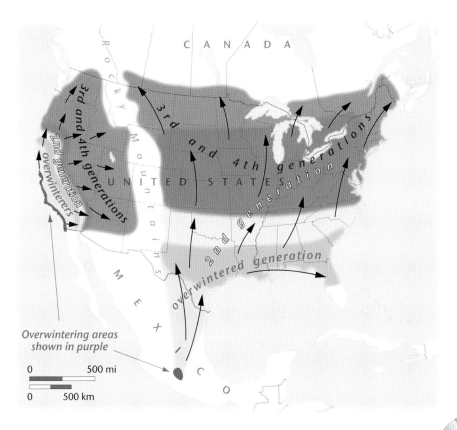

3rd and 4th generations

3rd and 4th generations

2nd generation overwinterers

3rd and 4th generation

2nd generation

overwintered generation

C A N A D A

Rocky Mountains

UNITED STATES

MEXICO

Overwintering areas
shown in purple

| 0 | 500 mi |
| 0 | 500 km |

In spring, the monarchs fly north. The ones in Mexico fly into the southern U.S., where they lay their eggs and die. In a few weeks, the adults emerge, and this new generation of butterflies flies farther north. The next two or three generations continue to move north. The last generation at the end of summer is different. It flies south before winter arrives.

Scientists are just starting to understand how butter-flies navigate. Butterflies have a magnetic compass in their brains that gives them a sense of direction. They have another compass that uses the sun's position to keep them on course. Their internal clock, which tells them what time of day it is, helps too. But that's not all. They may use landmarks to stay on track when they drift off course in the wind. Amazingly, they find their way back to where their great grandmother roosted the year before.

A hungry bird nabs a butterfly to eat. Birds, like this jacamar, learn quickly what to eat and what to avoid.

LOOKS MATTER

Butterflies are smaller than many animals, and they can't fight off birds and other predators. But that doesn't mean they are defenseless. They use tricks to avoid being eaten. Some play dead. Some have fake eyes (spots on their wings that look like eyes) to scare predators. Others have a false head at the end of their wings that tricks predators into attacking the wrong end. This strategy can help the butterfly escape.

Some butterflies use camouflage to blend in

Camouflage protects the yellow brimstone butterfly (Anteos maerula) among the leaves and flowers of a bush in Gomez Farias, Mexico.

HOW TO ATTRACT BUTTERFLIES

— Plant nectar plants (such as butterfly weed or butterfly bush).

— Plant host plants for the caterpillars to feed on.

— Put out a butterfly feeder.

with their environment. Some look like green leaves. Others are brown and look like dead leaves. Not only are these butterflies hard to see, but they usually fly very fast and not on a straight path. This makes them hard to catch!

Other butterflies are brightly colored. They can't really blend in. So how do they protect themselves? Many of them taste bad or are even poisonous, and birds learn not to eat them. The colors of these

↑ *These butterflies and moths belong to the tiger mimicry group. They were all collected from the same area of Costa Rica. Each one is a different species, yet they bear a very similar color pattern on their wings.*

so-called toxic butterflies often combine black with red, yellow, or orange. Toxic butterflies usually fly more slowly than nontoxic ones. Their colors, together with the way they fly, warn a predator, "don't touch." Some butterflies that don't taste bad look a lot like the ones that do, so predators stay away from them too.

Look-alike butterflies are called mimics. Even people can be fooled by them. I was in Mission, Texas, near the Mexican border when I heard about a butterfly

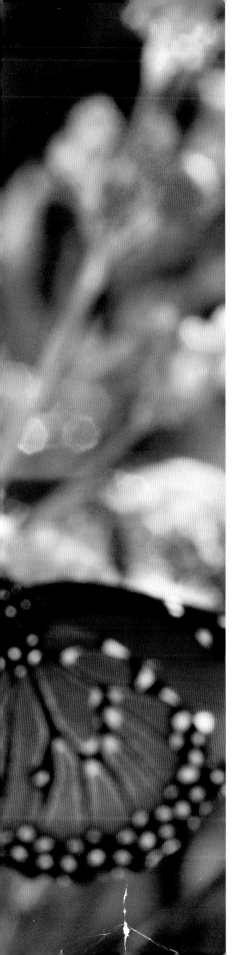

◀ Monarchs? No, take a closer look and compare them to the photo on page 17. The one in front is called a soldier, and the others are queens. They were visiting a butterfly garden planted by children in southern Texas.

garden planted by children and their parents. People said that lots of monarchs were visiting the garden. I went to the Mims School to see for myself.

It was an early morning in November, and sunlight was just entering the courtyard. The place came alive as swarms of orange and black butterflies descended on the flowering plants for a drink. I thought it could be the tail end of the monarch migration. But no! The monarchs had already migrated south to Mexico. These were queens and soldiers, species that mimic the monarch. Like the monarchs, their larvae feed on milkweed, and they taste bad to birds.

More and more schools are planting butterfly gardens like this one. Many plants and animals, including butterflies, are losing their habitats to human development, so by planting gardens, children are helping these creatures survive. I believe we can all pitch in to help butterflies. We can make our world a better and more beautiful place to live.

HOW YOU CAN HELP

Butterflies are among the most beautiful of all creatures. They also play an important role in nature. They pollinate flowering plants, and they serve as food for many animals. Sadly, butterflies face many challenges to their survival, including pollution, pesticides, and habitat loss. The good news is that you can help butterflies. The first step is to learn all you can about them. Read and watch videos about them—this book is a good start! Visit a live butterfly exhibit or an insect zoo, where you can watch butterflies. Tell your friends and relatives about what you learn. They might want to start helping butterflies, too!

■■■ Go outside and search for butterflies. Use a field guide to identify the butterflies that live in your area. Learn about them.

■■■ Ask your parents and neighbors to avoid using chemical pesticides in their gardens or yards. Pesticides can kill caterpillars as well as butterflies and other important pollinators.

■■■ Provide habitat for butterflies by planting a butterfly garden in your yard. Choose host plants and nectar plants to attract butterflies. For example, monarch butterflies use milkweed as a host plant, and they drink nectar from flowers such as lantana, black-eyed susan, and butterfly bush.

■■■ Try to organize the creation of a butterfly garden at your school. Enlist help from teachers, parents and friends.

■■■ Join with classmates, teachers, parents, and friends to plan a butterfly festival that will take place during the monarch migration. Find out when the butterflies tend to fly through your area. Celebrate their arrival with games and art projects, butterfly costumes, and "nectar" (fruit juice!) to drink. You could also collect milkweed seeds in the fall and give out the seeds or seedlings at the festival. You can do a lot to help people learn about the threats to monarchs and other species and help save them.

⬇ *A tiny red-bordered metalmark* (Caria ino) *sits on my fingertip.*

IT'S YOUR TURN

Once you begin to look for butterflies, you'll be amazed at how often you'll see them. They can be found in gardens, in the woods, in open fields, on mountaintops, in wetlands, in deserts—even on weeds in vacant lots. Watch quietly and patiently and take notes the next time you go exploring. Draw sketches of the butterflies you see. If you have close-focusing binoculars, use them to get a better look. Try taking pictures of butterflies. Start keeping a journal of the butterflies you encounter nearby or while you're on trips. Here are things to note about them:

▬ Size.

▬ Wing shape. Are the forewings (top wings) rounded or pointy? Are the edges of the hind (or bottom) wing jagged, smooth, or scalloped? Does the butterfly have a "tail" on the hind wings?

▬ Colors and patterns. Is there any iridescence (a play of colors like you see in a soap bubble)?

▬ Activity. What is it doing?

▬ Location. Where is it?

▬ Other details. Does it have eye spots on the wings?

▬ Flight style. Does it fly slowly and in a straight line, or very fast and in a zigzag manner?

▬ Mimicry. Does it look like any other butterflies in your field guide?

⬇ *With distinct eyespots on its forewings, this blue metalmark butterfly* (Mesosemia asa) *looks like it's staring at us.*

FACTS AT A GLANCE

⬇ *A green longwing (Philaethria dido)* hangs upside down by its feet to catch a good night's sleep.

Common and Scientific Names

Butterflies are part of a larger group (or order) of insects called the Lepidoptera. True butterflies are part of the superfamily Papilionoidea.

Size

Butterflies range in size from about one-half inch (1.3 cm) across the wings to about 12 inches (30.5 cm). The Queen Alexandra's birdwing is the largest butterfly. The female, which is larger than the male, can measure up to 12 inches across. In the United States, the largest butterfly is the giant swallowtail. It has a maximum wingspan of 6 inches (15.2 cm). The smallest butterfly is the western pygmy blue. It measures about one-half inch.

Life Cycle

Butterflies move through four stages as they grow up: the egg, the caterpillar (larva), the pupa (chrysalis), and the adult (imago).

Life Span

Most adult butterflies live for only a week or two, but some, like passion vine butterflies, may live almost a year. Other life cycle stages can last from a few weeks to a year or more.

Diet

Adult butterflies have a liquid diet that can include nectar, rotting fruit, liquefied pollen, water, sweat, urine, dung, carrion, and tree sap. A butterfly's diet depends on its species.

Number of Species

About 17,000 species of butterflies and 145,000 species of moths have been given a scientific name. Many are yet unnamed. Included with true butterflies are the sister groups: skippers (with more than 3,500 species) and American moth butterflies (with 35 recognized species).

Range and Habitat

Butterflies are found on every continent except Antarctica. Some species occur over a very large area (like the painted lady and monarch). Others live in a very limited area. Habitats range from forests to treeless regions to wetlands. Butterfly habitats depend on the species of butterfly, the presence of appropriate food plants for adults and caterpillars, and a favorable climate. Predators, parasites, and competing species can also influence a butterfly's presence or absence in a given habitat.

Physical Characteristics

Butterflies have six legs and three body segments: the head, thorax, and abdomen. Two sets of wings (the forewing and hind wing) are attached to the thorax. Butterflies have an outer skeleton (the exoskeleton) that supports them. Like most insects, adult butterflies, as well as caterpillars and pupae, breathe through air holes in their bodies called spiracles

Senses

Butterflies see with large compound eyes, taste with their proboscis and the tips of their feet, and smell with their antennae. Most butterflies do not hear but are able to feel sound vibrations through the veins of their wings. They have sensory hairs over most of their bodies that sense touch. Some of these hairs are specialized and can sense wind, gravity, and the position of their body.

Differences Between Butterflies and Moths

The main differences are seen in the adults. The easiest part to identify is the antennae. They are knobbed at the tips in butterflies and are either feathery or straight in moths. Butterflies fly during the day. Most moths fly at night. At rest, butterflies close their wings over their backs. Moths hold their wings open or in another position.

Special Features

At any stage in their life cycle, butterflies can go through a resting phase, called diapause. Growth and development cease during diapause, which helps the butterfly survive extreme temperatures, drought, or lack of food. Some desert-dwelling species of yucca moths can remain as pupae for over 30 years before turning into adults! Monarchs are great navigators.

They have a built-in magnetic compass, a sun compass, an internal clock to adjust for time of day, and an ability to use landmarks to stay on course.

Biggest Threats

The most serious threats to butterflies are caused by humans. Butterfly habitats are being destroyed for logging and farming, and to make way for roads and human settlements. Very large amounts of pesticides and herbicides are used in most farming. Pesticides kill not only pests, but butterflies too. Herbicides kill plants (other than crops) including butterfly host plants and nectar plants. Pollen from corn whose genes have been altered to kill pests can also kill caterpillars. Pollution is harmful too. Certain species of butterflies have gone extinct because of human activities, and some others are in danger of extinction. Illegal logging in Mexico is destroying the forests where the eastern monarchs roost during winter.

GLOSSARY

Abdomen: The rear segment of an insect's body, which contains organs for digestion and reproduction.

Antennae: Feelers on an insect's head that help it smell, feel, and taste.

Camouflage: Concealment; using shape or coloration to blend in with one's surroundings.

Carrion: Dead animal flesh.

Caterpillar: The larval stage of a butterfly or moth.

Chrysalis: A butterfly pupa.

Compound eye: An eye made of many lenses that form multiple images.

Dung: Animal droppings.

Eyespots: Bold, circular markings on an insect that resemble large eyes.

Host plant: A plant that caterpillars eat. Butterflies lay eggs on a host plant.

Life cycle: The different stages in an organism's life. The first stage is when life begins and the final stage happens when the organism can reproduce and have young.

Mating: When an adult male and female come together to produce young.

Metamorphosis: A change in shape and habits, such as when a caterpillar becomes a butterfly.

Migration: The seasonal movement of animals from one place to another.

Molting: The action of shedding.

Nectar: A sugary liquid that flowers produce.

Pollination: The process in which pollen is transferred from one flower to another of the same species to fertilize it.

Predator: An animal that hunts and kills other animals for food.

Proboscis: The flexible tube of a butterfly or moth, used for sucking nectar.

Pupa: The resting stage of an insect as it transforms from larva to adult.

Roost: A tree or other place where animals rest or sleep.

Species: A group of living things that look like one another and are able to reproduce with each other.

Thorax: The middle segment of an insect's body, to which its legs and wings are attached.

Toxic: Poisonous or harmful.

FIND OUT MORE

Books & Articles

"Living Color." *National Geographic Explorer* magazine, April 2009, pp. 2–7.

Murawski, Darlyne. *Face to Face with Caterpillars.* National Geographic, 2007.

Murawski, Darlyne, "A Taste for Poison: Passion Vine Butterflies." *National Geographic* magazine, Dec. 1993, pp. 122–137.

Opler, Paul, et al. *Peterson First Guide to Butterflies and Moths.* Houghton Mifflin, 1998.

Patent, Dorothy. *Fabulous Fluttering Tropical Butterflies.* Walker, 2003.

Ryder, Joanne, and Lynne Cherry. *Where Butterflies Grow.* Puffin, 1996.

Stewart, Doug, "Beauty with Brains." *National Wildlife* magazine, April/May 2004.

Web Sites

http://www.nababutterfly.com
The basics of butterfly gardening.

http://www.kidsbutterfly.org/
Butterfly and moth information.

http://www.butterfliesandmoths.org/
A chance to look up butterflies from your area.

http://magma.nationalgeographic.com/ngexplorer/0904/teachers.
Click on NG Kids Video: Monarch Butterflies. Watch a video about monarch butterfly migration.

http://www.monarchlab.umn.edu/
Monarch life cycle and more.

www.monarchwatch.org. With the help of an adult, you can follow the progress of the monarch migration.

INDEX

RESEARCH & PHOTOGRAPHIC NOTES

When butterflies see you coming, they quickly fly away, so the best way to photograph them is to sneak up very slowly and not make any fast moves. When they are busily drinking nectar, they might stay a little longer.

I'd compare photographing butterflies to photographing sports. You need a quick trigger finger to get your shot. The eggs, caterpillars, and pupae, of course, are much easier than adults to photograph. The eggs are very, very small, and I use special equipment, including macro lenses, to get that close.

A few years after I finished my research in Costa Rica, I returned to the same site to photograph the passion vine butterflies for my first article for *National Geographic* magazine (Dec. 1993). The butterflies are not very common in the rain forest, but from my research I already knew where to find the host plants and their favorite flowers. I also knew what time of day the butterflies would visit certain places. Otherwise it would have been much harder to get the photographs I wanted. There is no substitute for firsthand field experience.

Hummingbirds would occasionally visit the same flowers as the butterflies. One time while I was observing a butterfly on a flower, a hummingbird speared a hole right through its wings. The hummingbird wouldn't let any butterflies take nectar from the flowers. Rare moments like that are almost impossible to capture on camera unless you know ahead of time that it might happen. Then you can set up and wait for the moment.

I shot most of the photos in this book with film. I now prefer digital photography because I can see the results instantly and because I'm able to photograph in low-light situations. I like to photograph butterflies wherever I go, but I don't need to go very far to find them. A few of the photos in this book were taken close to home in Massachusetts.

FOR HELEN, BRUCE, GRACE,
AND FOR ALL CHILDREN WHO
LOVE BUTTERFLIES.

Acknowledgments
I'm very grateful to all who have provided information or made it possible to shoot the photos for this book, especially Ruben Canet, Rod Eastwood, Lawrence E. Gilbert, and all who participated in the mark and recapture program of *Heliconius* butterflies; Mauricio Linares; Don Harvey; Keith Willmott, Luis Miguel Constantino; Becky Rebentisch; Michael and Janie Maurer, the children from the Mims School, their parents, and their teacher, Lou Anne Bell; the National Parks of Costa Rica; the Smithsonian Tropical Research Institute; the Bentsen-Rio Grande Valley State Park; ANCON (Asociatión Nacional para la Conservación de la Naturaleza) in Panama; Butterfly World in Coconut Creek, Florida; and the Butterfly Place in Westford, Massachusetts.

The publisher gratefully acknowledges the assistance of Christine Kiel, K-3 curriculum and reading consultant, and Lincoln Brower, for his assistance with the maps and review of the text.

Book design by David M. Seager.
The body text of the book is set in ITC Century. The display text is set in Knockout and Party Noid.

Published by the National Geographic Society

John M. Fahey, Jr., *President and Chief Executive Officer*

Gilbert M. Grosvenor, *Chairman of the Board*

Tim T. Kelly, *President, Global Media Group*

John Q. Griffin, *President, Publishing*

Nina D. Hoffman, *Executive Vice President; President, Book Publishing Group*

Melina Gerosa Bellows, *Executive Vice President, Children's Publishing*

Staff for This Book

Nancy Laties Feresten, *Vice President, Editor-in-Chief of Children's Books*

Jonathan Halling, *Design Director, Children's Publishing*

Priyanka Lamichhane, Mary Beth Oelkers-Keegan, *Project Editors*

David M. Seager, *Art Director*

Lori Epstein, *Illustrations Editor*

M.F. Delano, *Researcher*

Carl Mehler, *Director of Maps*

Sven M. Dolling, *Map Editor*

Kate Olesin, *Editorial Assistant*

Jennifer Thornton, *Managing Editor*

Grace Hill, *Associate Managing Editor*

R. Gary Colbert, *Production Director*

Lewis R. Bassford, *Production Manager*

Rachel Faulise, Nicole Elliott, *Manufacturing Managers*

Susan Borke, *Legal and Business Affairs*

Front cover: Face to face with a monarch butterfly; front flap: The proboscis on this passion vine butterfly is covered in pollen; back cover: A dazzling blue morpho butterfly sits on Darlyne Murawski's finger. Title page: A red-spotted cattleheart rests on a leaf.

Library of Congress
Cataloging-in-Publication Data

Murawski, Darlyne.
 Face to face with butterflies / by Darlyne A. Murawski. -- 1st ed.
      p. cm.
 Includes bibliographical references and index.
 ISBN 978-1-4263-0618-1 (hardcover : alk. paper) -- ISBN 978-1-4263-0619-8 (library binding : alk. paper)
 1. Butterflies--Juvenile literature. I. Title.

QL544.2.M865 2010
595.78'9--dc22
                        2009031723

Founded in 1888, the National Geographic Society is one of the largest nonprofit scientific and educational organizations in the world. It reaches more than 285 million people worldwide each month through its official journal, NATIONAL GEOGRAPHIC, and its four other magazines; the National Geographic Channel; television documentaries; radio programs; films; books; videos and DVDs; maps; and interactive media. National Geographic has funded more than 8,000 scientific research projects and supports an education program combating geographic illiteracy.

For more information, please call 1-800-NGS LINE (647-5463) or write to the following address:
National Geographic Society
1145 17th Street N.W.
Washington, D.C. 20036-4688 U.S.A.

Visit us online at www.nationalgeographic.com/books. Librarians and teachers, visit us at www.ngchildrensbooks.org. Kids and parents, visit us at kids.nationalgeographic.com.

For information about special discounts for bulk purchases, please contact National Geographic Books Special Sales: ngspecsales@ngs.org.

For rights or permissions inquiries, please contact National Geographic Books Subsidiary Rights: ngbookrights@ngs.org.

Printed in China.

10/RRDS/1